# WILD about
# PLANES

## By Bill Gunston

## Stats and Facts • Top makes • Top models • Top speeds

# WILD about
# PLANES

Copyright © *ticktock* Entertainment Ltd 2003
First published in Great Britain in 2003 by *ticktock* Media Ltd.,
Unit 2, Orchard Business Centre, North Farm Road, Tunbridge Wells, Kent, TN2 3XF
We would like to thank: Sam Petter, Keith Faulkner of Jane's Defence Weekly and Elizabeth Wiggans.
Picture Credits: Corbis: P4-5, P9b, P26-27.  Aviation Picture Library: P6-7, P8-9c, P10-11, P16-17, P18-19,
P20-21, P30-31. Lockheed: P22-23. NASA: P12-13, P24-25, P28-29. Skyscan: P14-15.
ISBN 1 86007 359 X HB
ISBN 1 86007 365 4 PB
Printed in China
A CIP catalogue record for this book is available from the British Library.

# CONTENTS

# AIRBUS A380

**DID YOU KNOW?**

*The A380-800F freighter will be used to carry heavy loads. It will carry up to 147 tonnes of cargo.*

Ever since the first plane took to the skies, aircraft have got bigger and bigger. In 1957 the American firm Boeing produced the enormous 707. Then in 1970, they launched the even bigger 747. In 2006, a new giant will start flying, the enormous Airbus A380.

The body of the A380 is deeper and wider than a 747. There are two **engines** on each **wing**.

Airbus's A380 monster looks a bit like a double decker 747 (see page 8-9).

The standard A380 has room for 854 passengers, while the stretched version can seat 1,000 people. On board the plane there will also be shopping malls, children's play areas and other facilities!

# STATS AND FACTS

**LAUNCHED:** *2006*

**ORIGIN:** *Europe*

**MODELS:** *Five passenger versions, and the A380-800F for cargo*

**ENGINES:** *Four Rolls-Royce Trent 900 engines providing 36,280 kg thrust or four Engine Alliance GP7200 turbofans, rated at 37,003 kg thrust*

**WINGSPAN:** *79.8 metres*

**LENGTH:** *73 metres*

**CREW:** *Two*

**SEATING:** *Up to 1,000*

**MAX SPEED:** *588 mph*

**MAX WEIGHT:** *590 tonnes*

**RANGE:** *9,378 miles*

**LOAD:** *Up to 1,000 passengers or 150 tonnes of cargo*

**COST:** *£154 million*

# SR-71 BLACKBIRD

In 1960 the USSR shot down a US spy plane. After this disaster the American military were ordered to make a craft that would never be shot down again. The result was the amazing SR-71, packed with cameras and **sensors**. In 20 years of dangerous missions, no Blackbird was ever lost in combat.

## DID YOU KNOW?

*The Blackbird once flew from New York–London in 1 hour 55 minutes.*

WARNING
Restricted Area

The Blackbird was made in top secrecy. President Johnson refused to admit that it even existed until 1964.

# STATS AND FACTS

**LAUNCHED:** *1962*

**ORIGIN:** *USA*

**MODELS:** *SR-71A, SR-71B and SR-71C*

**ENGINES:** *Two Pratt & Whitney J58-P-10s with afterburners, providing 14,724 kg thrust each*

**WINGSPAN:** *16.94 metres*

**LENGTH:** *31.65 metres*

**CREW:** *Two*

**MAX SPEED:** *2,250 mph (Mach 3.4)*

**MAX WEIGHT:** *78 tonnes*

**RANGE:** *3,000 miles*

**LOAD:** *Sensors and powerful cameras*

**COST:** *£33 million (in 1962)*

Each **engine** has enough **thrust** to power an ocean liner. The large spikes catch air to keep the plane balanced in flight.

The SR-71's are made of a special material called **titanium alloy**. It protects the planes from the extreme heat produced flying at such high speeds.

# BOEING 747

On 13th April 1966 the American aircraft maker Boeing received its first order for a new plane. It was the 747, also known as the **Jumbo** Jet. Boeing went on to sell an incredible 1,400 of these monsters, which cost a total of £175 billion.

## DID YOU KNOW?

*The wingspan of a Jumbo Jet is longer than the distance of the first manned flight.*

747's can carry up to 550 passengers. They were the first wide-body planes ever built, with two aisles along the **cabin**.

All 747s look similar. However modern Jumbos have far more powerful **engines** than early models.

## STATS AND FACTS

**LAUNCHED:** *1966*

**ORIGIN:** *USA*

**MODELS:** *747 -100, -200, -300, -400, 400F, -400LR*

**ENGINES:** *Four 25,855-28,123-kg thrust Pratt & Whitney, General Electric or Rolls-Royce turbofans*

**WINGSPAN:** *Up to 64.92 metres*

**LENGTH:** *Up to 70.67 metres*

**CREW:** *Two active pilots, two resting pilots and up to 25 cabin staff*

**MAX SPEED:** *Up to 561 mph*

**MAX WEIGHT:** *417.7 tonnes*

**RANGE:** *8,681 miles*

**LOAD:** *550 passengers or 113 tonnes of cargo*

**COST:** *£14 million (in 1966)*

The 747-400F model can load containers weighing up to 113 tonnes through its **nose**.

# B-2 SPIRIT

**Stealth technology** has developed very quickly. By 1978 it was possible to design an aircraft that was almost invisible to **radar**. One of the most striking of these planes was the B-2. The first model flew in July 1989, and looked like it came from another planet.

## DID YOU KNOW?

*The B-2's skin is jet black and smooth. All the joints are carefully concealed.*

The B-2 is really just a giant **wing** with sharp edges. The strange bulges hide the plane's **engines**, **cockpit** and bombs.

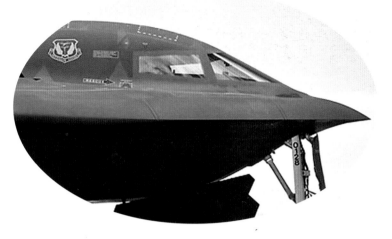

The plane has just two crew on board. The rest of the cockpit is taken up by computer-controlled flight equipment.

## STATS AND FACTS

**LAUNCHED:** *1989*

**ORIGIN:** *USA*

**MODELS:** *The US Air Force has 20 planes, all slightly different*

**ENGINES:** *Four General Electric F118-GE-110 turbofans each rated at 8,618 kg thrust*

**WINGSPAN:** *52.43 metres*

**LENGTH:** *21.03 metres*

**CREW:** *Two*

**MAX SPEED:** *630 mph*

**MAX WEIGHT:** *181.4 tonnes*

**RANGE:** *7,644 miles*

**LOAD:** *Up to 22.6 tonnes of many types of nuclear or conventional bombs, missiles or mines*

**COST:** *£1.6 billion*

The B-2 is stuffed full of computers and heat and noise reducing technology. It is the world's most expensive aircraft. In 1998 each plane cost an amazing £1.6 billion!

# B-52 STRATOFORTRESS

After World War 2, the US Air Force decided to create huge aircraft that would put people off starting wars. They were called the B-52's, and were monster eight-**engined** jet bombers. In 1952 the first of these giants took to the skies.

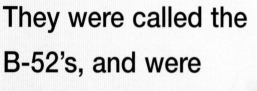

## DID YOU KNOW?

*There are six ejection seats on a B-52 in case of emergency.*

The B-52 has **sensors** that let the plane fly very close to the ground during combat missions.

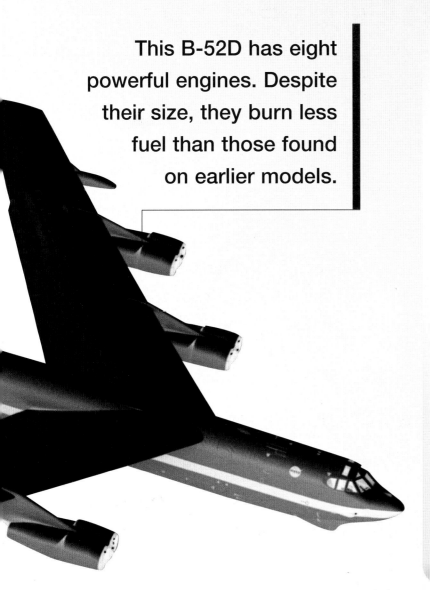

This B-52D has eight powerful engines. Despite their size, they burn less fuel than those found on earlier models.

# STATS AND FACTS

**LAUNCHED:** *1952*

**ORIGIN:** *USA*

**MODELS:** *XB-52, YB-52 (1952), B-52A to B-52H (1954-65)*

**ENGINES:** *Eight 7,711 kg thrust Pratt & Whitney TF33 turbofan engines*

**WINGSPAN:** *56.39 metres*

**LENGTH:** *49.05 metres*

**CREW:** *Six*

**MAX SPEED:** *595 mph*

**MAX WEIGHT:** *256.7 tonnes*

**RANGE:** *12,566 miles*

**LOAD:** *Nuclear or high-explosive bombs, cruise missiles and a variety of guns*

**COST:** *£6 million (in 1952)*

This B-52 is being refuelled in flight. **Air refuelling** allows B-52s to fly almost anywhere in the world.

# CONCORDE

In 1962 Britain and France decided to build a plane that would cut the time of long journeys. Concorde cruises at **Mach** 2 – twice the speed of sound. This amazing plane cuts the time it takes to fly from London to New York to just over three hours.

## DID YOU KNOW?

*When it is in flight, Concorde heats up the air around it. This heat causes the plane to expand!*

Concorde's slim body and paper-dart shape means it can fly more than twice as fast as any other passenger plane.

## STATS AND FACTS

**LAUNCHED:** *1977*

**ORIGIN:** *Britain/France*

**MODELS:** *Only one production type, which is larger than prototypes*

**ENGINES:** *Four Rolls-Royce/ Snecma Olympus S93 turbojets, providing 17,260 kg thrust*

**WINGSPAN:** *25.6 metres*

**LENGTH:** *62.18 metres*

**CREW:** *Two pilots*

**MAX SPEED:** *1,350 mph (Mach 2)*

**MAX WEIGHT:** *185 tonnes*

**RANGE:** *4,509 miles*

**LOAD:** *Room for 140 passengers, but usually seats 100*

**COST:** *£23 million (in 1977)*

To let the **pilot** see ahead when landing Concorde's entire **nose** hinges down. A part of the windscreen also folds into the nose.

The power required for takeoff is provided by Concorde's four **engines**. The plane can reach 225 mph in just 30 seconds.

# EUROFIGHTER TYPHOON

European countries get together to develop new warplanes. For each partner this is cheaper than developing an aircraft by themselves. The latest example is the Typhoon, developed by Britain, Germany, Italy and Spain.

## DID YOU KNOW?

*The idea for a Eurofighter dates back to 1979. However, it was over 20 years before the first Typhoon was built.*

Only 15% of the outside of the Eurofighter's body is made of metal. The rest is mainly lightweight **carbon fibre** that lets it cruise at great speeds without overheating.

# STATS AND FACTS

**LAUNCHED:** *2002*

**ORIGIN:** *Europe*

**MODELS:** *Single seat and two seat versions*

**ENGINES:** *Two Eurojet EJ200 reheated turbofans each providing 9,072 kg thrust*

**WINGSPAN:** *10.95 metres*

**LENGTH:** *15.96 metres*

**CREW:** *One or two*

**MAX SPEED:** *1,323 mph (Mach 2)*

**MAX WEIGHT:** *21 tonnes*

**RANGE:** *1,800 miles*

**LOAD:** *One 27-mm gun (not used by UK) and up to 8 tonnes of missiles or bombs on 13 attachments*

**COST:** *£20 million*

The Typhoon has two **engines**. It also has a large triangular **wing** and small powered **foreplanes** on each side of the nose. The Typhoon comes in one or two seat versions.

The twin engines allow the Typhoon to accelerate to **Mach** 1 – the speed of sound – in under 30 seconds. The Typhoon can also take off in just five seconds!

# F-117A Nighthawk

First flown in 1981, the F-117A is perhaps the weirdest aircraft ever made. Its shape is designed to break up enemy **radar** signals. Because it can be **air refuelled**, the F-117A can travel almost anywhere in the world. This amazing plane is made by the US firm Lockheed.

**DID YOU KNOW?**

*The only non-black parts of the F-117A are the windows.*

The F-117A is made up of hundreds of flat surfaces. These deflect enemy **radar** and make the plane almost invisible.

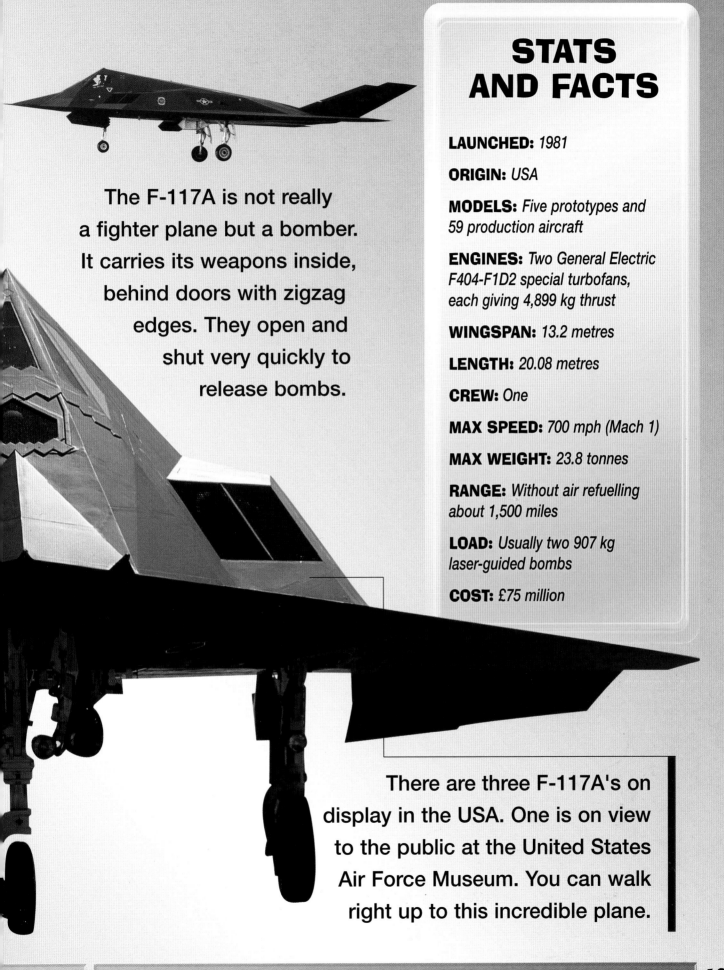

The F-117A is not really a fighter plane but a bomber. It carries its weapons inside, behind doors with zigzag edges. They open and shut very quickly to release bombs.

## STATS AND FACTS

**LAUNCHED:** *1981*

**ORIGIN:** *USA*

**MODELS:** *Five prototypes and 59 production aircraft*

**ENGINES:** *Two General Electric F404-F1D2 special turbofans, each giving 4,899 kg thrust*

**WINGSPAN:** *13.2 metres*

**LENGTH:** *20.08 metres*

**CREW:** *One*

**MAX SPEED:** *700 mph (Mach 1)*

**MAX WEIGHT:** *23.8 tonnes*

**RANGE:** *Without air refuelling about 1,500 miles*

**LOAD:** *Usually two 907 kg laser-guided bombs*

**COST:** *£75 million*

There are three F-117A's on display in the USA. One is on view to the public at the United States Air Force Museum. You can walk right up to this incredible plane.

# HARRIER

By the end of the 1950s air forces started asking for planes that could operate from backyards, forest clearings or even small ships. To meet this need, Hawker Aircraft in England launched one of the first **VTOL** (vertical takeoff and landing) aircraft in 1969. This plane was called the Harrier.

## DID YOU KNOW?

*The US Marine Corps use the Harrier to provide air power for a force invading an enemy shore.*

This single-seat Sea Harrier operates from ships. There are also two-seater versions and trainer versions.

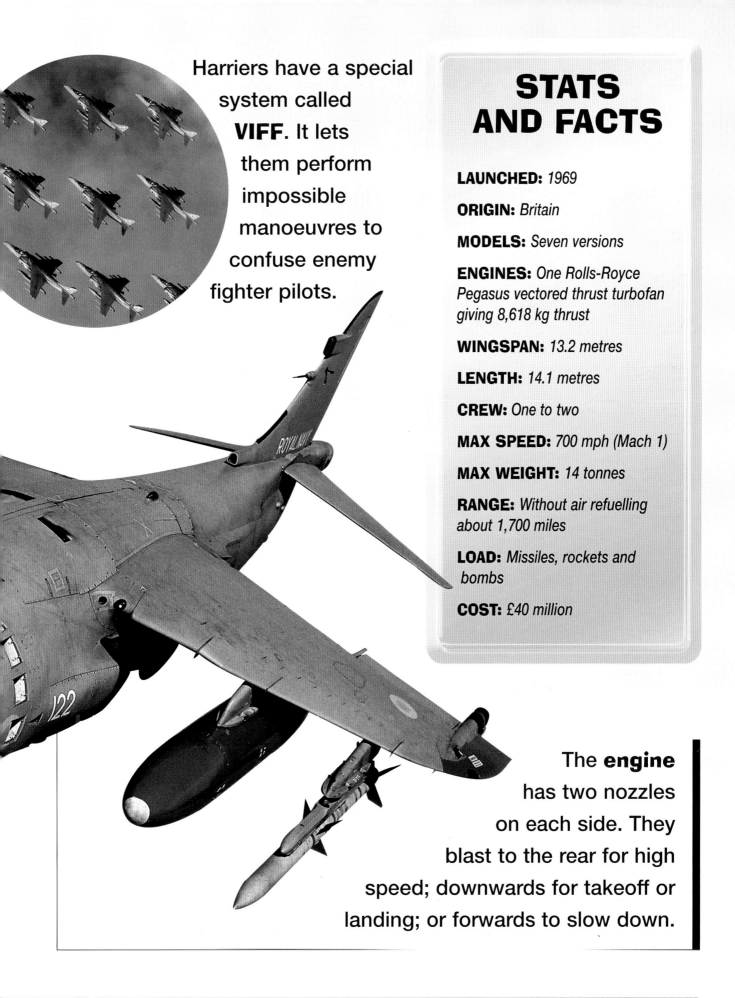

Harriers have a special system called **VIFF**. It lets them perform impossible manoeuvres to confuse enemy fighter pilots.

## STATS AND FACTS

**LAUNCHED:** *1969*

**ORIGIN:** *Britain*

**MODELS:** *Seven versions*

**ENGINES:** *One Rolls-Royce Pegasus vectored thrust turbofan giving 8,618 kg thrust*

**WINGSPAN:** *13.2 metres*

**LENGTH:** *14.1 metres*

**CREW:** *One to two*

**MAX SPEED:** *700 mph (Mach 1)*

**MAX WEIGHT:** *14 tonnes*

**RANGE:** *Without air refuelling about 1,700 miles*

**LOAD:** *Missiles, rockets and bombs*

**COST:** *£40 million*

The **engine** has two nozzles on each side. They blast to the rear for high speed; downwards for takeoff or landing; or forwards to slow down.

# JOINT STRIKE FIGHTER

In 1995 the USAF and US Navy launched a programme for a JSF (Joint Strike Fighter). Their aim was to produce the next generation of advanced planes for airfields and aircraft carriers.

## DID YOU KNOW?

*While the original partners expect to buy 3,002 F-35s, sales to other countries are likely to double this total.*

All JSF models carry weapons in two bays on each side of the **fuselage**.

The rear **exhaust** produces **thrust** to lift the aircraft. The X-35B is given extra lift by a fan that takes power from the engine.

## STATS AND FACTS

**LAUNCHED:** *1995*

**ORIGIN:** *USA*

**MODELS:** *X-35A, X-35B and X-35C, described below*

**ENGINES:** *One Pratt & Whitney F135 turbofan delivering 18,144 kg thrust, with one Rolls-Royce Allison engine-driven lift fan on the X-35B*

**WINGSPAN:** *Up to 13.26 metres*

**LENGTH:** *15.39 metres*

**CREW:** *One*

**MAX SPEED:** *1,058 mph (Mach 1.6)*

**MAX WEIGHT:** *27.2 tonnes*

**RANGE:** *About 1,380 miles*

**LOAD:** *Enormous variety of guns, missiles and bombs up to 7.7 tonnes*

**COST:** *£66 million*

There are three versions of the JSF. The X-35A is the basic version. The X-35B comes with a more powerful **engine**. The X-35C (*left*) has a bigger **wing**, which can fold.

# SPACE SHUTTLE

The first space flights relied on rockets, giant tubes which stood upright and were fired into orbit. Then in April 1981 the Shuttle was launched. It was the first spacecraft that could be brought back to Earth.

Enterprise

United States

NASA

## DID YOU KNOW?

*The Shuttle's boosters fall off into the sea. They are recovered and used again.*

At the front is an area for up to ten crew, including two **pilots**. In the middle is a large **bay** for **satellites**. At the back are three big rocket **engines**.

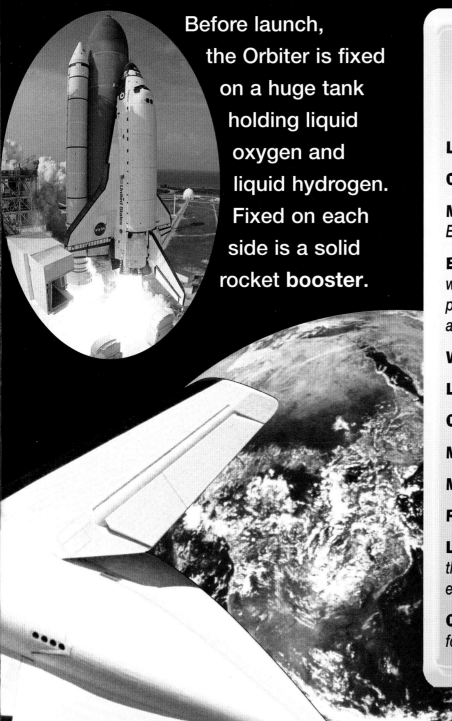

Before launch, the Orbiter is fixed on a huge tank holding liquid oxygen and liquid hydrogen. Fixed on each side is a solid rocket **booster**.

## STATS AND FACTS

**LAUNCHED:** *1981*

**ORIGIN:** *USA*

**MODELS:** *Discovery, Atlantis, Endeavour and Colombia*

**ENGINES:** *Three orbiter engines with combined thrust of 540,000 kg, plus two solid–rocket boosters with a combined thrust of 2,610,000 kg*

**WINGSPAN:** *23.79 metres*

**LENGTH:** *56.14 metres*

**CREW:** *Up to ten*

**MAX SPEED:** *17,440 mph*

**MAX WEIGHT:** *2.041 tonnes*

**RANGE:** *116-403 miles*

**LOAD:** *Satellites, components for the joint space station and space experiments*

**COST:** *£1.25 billion plus £294 million for each launch*

After the mission the Shuttle returns to Earth. It is protected by heat-resistant tiles. The Shuttle glides without engine power onto a runway, and is slowed down by a big **parachute**.

# VOYAGER

On 23rd December 1986 a strange looking airplane landed at Edwards Air Force Base, California. It had taken off from the same runway nine days previously and flown round the world non-stop. This had never been done before.

## DID YOU KNOW?

*During its epic journey, Voyager covered 24,986 miles non-stop.*

The Voyager was flown by two people. They laid down in a tiny space with a **propeller** at each end. The body was fixed on the centre of a fantastic **wing**.

Voyager was made from **carbon fibre** and **glass fibre**. At rest, its wings scraped on the ground, but in flight they curved upwards like the wings of a bird.

# STATS AND FACTS

**LAUNCHED:** *1985*

**ORIGIN:** *USA*

**MODELS:** *One*

**ENGINES:** *Two Teledyne Continental engines (front 130 bhp, rear 110 bhp)*

**WINGSPAN:** *33.77 metres*

**LENGTH:** *8.9 metres*

**CREW:** *Two*

**MAXIMUM SPEED:** *122 mph*

**MAXIMUM WEIGHT:** *4.4 tonnes*

**RANGE:** *27,455 miles*

**LOAD:** *Two crew*

**COST:** *£1 million*

The Voyager was one of many weird looking airplanes created by Bert Rutan. It was flown around the world by his brother Dick, with co-pilot Jeana Yeager.

# X-43A

## DID YOU KNOW?

*Before the X-43A came the amazing X-15. It reached an unbeaten speed of 4,534 mph (Mach 6.87) during several flights.*

NASA (National Air and Space Administration) is best known for making space rockets. It also carries out important research into aircraft. The X-43A is one of the latest research planes. It is used to find out the best shape to fly at very high speeds in the upper part of the atmosphere.

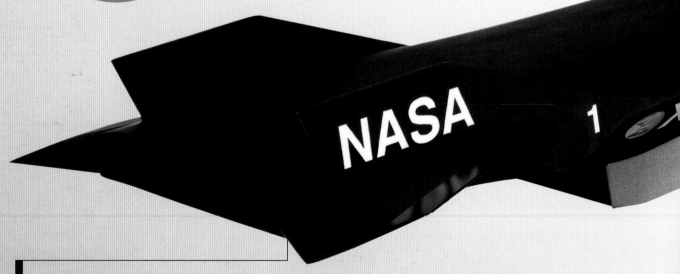

The X-43A has a wide bottom, flat top and two fins. It is powered by a powerful **Scramjet** engine, which burns hydrogen-based fuel.

When launched, the X-43 will travel at between **Mach** 7 and Mach 10, or 4,620–6,600 mph. This means it could travel from London to New York in just 40 minutes, a journey that usually takes seven hours!

# STATS AND FACTS

**LAUNCHED:** *2001 (test version)*

**ORIGIN:** *USA*

**MODELS:** *Three test models, each slightly different*

**ENGINE:** *GASL hydrogen-fuelled scramjet engine*

**WINGSPAN:** *1.5 metres*

**LENGTH:** *3.66 metres*

**CREW:** *Unmanned at present*

**MAX SPEED:** *6,600 mph (Mach 10)*

**MAX WEIGHT:** *1.3 tonnes*

**RANGE:** *Unknown*

**COST:** *£250 million*

The X-43A's first flight took place on 2 June 2001. It was dropped from a B-52 over the Pacific Ocean. However, the plane broke up in the sky, and NASA is still trying to work out what went wrong.

# GLOSSARY

**AFTERBURNER** System which injects extra fuel into the exhaust gases of a plane to provide large amounts of extra power.

**AIR REFUELLING** Method of refuelling military aircraft whilst in flight, via a fuel hose linked to a tanker aircraft.

**BOOSTERS** Large canisters containing fuel that are attached to the sides of a space rocket as it is launched.

**CABIN** The enclosed space in an aircraft or spacecraft that holds the crew, passengers and cargo.

**CARBON/GLASS FIBRE** A modern strong, but lightweight material.

**COCKPIT** The part of an aircraft where the pilot and his assistants sit.

**EJECTION SEAT** A seat, usually fitted in military aircraft, that can be fired or ejected from the aircraft.

**ENGINE** The part of a plane where fuel is burned to create energy.

**EXHAUSTS** Pipes at the back of a plane that let out poisonous gases made when fuel is burned.

**FOREPLANES** Moveable surfaces at the front of a plane that provide extra lift and balance.

**FREIGHTER** An aircraft made to carry cargo rather than passengers.

**FUSELAGE** *See Cabin*.

**HOLD** The lower part of a plane where cargo is stored.

**JETS** Part of an engine that provides the lifting power for an aircraft.

**JUMBO** Another name for a Boeing 747.

**LASER GUIDED BOMB** A bomb launched from an aircraft that has sensors in its nose to guide it onto a target.

**MACH** Measurement which relates the speed of an aircraft to the speed of sound. Mach 1 is the speed of sound (700 mph); Mach 2 is twice the speed of sound.

**NOSE** The rounded front of an aircraft.

**ORBITER** A spacecraft or satellite designed to orbit a planet or other body without landing on it.

**PARACHUTE** A large canopy with a body harness underneath. It is designed to slow the rate of descent of a person from an aircraft.

**PILOT** A person qualified to fly an aircraft or spaceship.

**PROPELLER** A machine with spinning blades that provides thrust to lift an aircraft.

**RADAR** A method of detecting distant objects using radio waves.

**SCRAMJET** A hydrogen-fuelled engine designed for flying at five times the speed of sound.

**SENSORS** Devices that help pilots fly their aircraft, detect enemy aircraft, or fire weapons accurately.

**STEALTH TECHNOLOGY** Technology used to make a plane almost invisible.

**SUPERSONIC** Faster than the speed of sound.

**TAIL** The rear part of the fuselage that balances a plane.

**THRUST** A pushing force created in a jet engine or rocket that gives aircraft enough speed to take off.

**TITANIUM ALLOY** A light, strong and heat-tolerant material.

**TURBOFAN** An engine with a fan used to boost an engine's power.

**TURBINE** Machine with a wheel or rotor driven by water, steam or gases.

**VTOL** Vertical Take-Off, Vertical Landing. System that holds an aircraft in the air as it takes off or lands.

**VIFF** Vectoring in Forward Flight. System that lets a plane change direction very suddenly.

**WINGSPAN** The distance between the tips of the wings of an aircraft.

**WINGS** Part of the aircraft that provides lift, placed on either side of the fuselage.

# INDEX